# When God Comes Down

## An Advent Study for Adults

## JAMES A. HARNISH

*Abingdon Press*
*Nashville*

WHEN GOD COMES DOWN
AN ADVENT STUDY FOR ADULTS
Copyright © 2012 by Abingdon Press

*This book is printed on acid-free paper.*

**Library of Congress Cataloging-in-Publication Data**

Harnish, James A.
  When God comes down : an Advent study for adults / James A. Harnish.
     p. cm.
  Includes bibliographical references and index.
  ISBN 978-1-4267-5108-0 (pbk. : alk. paper) 1. Advent 2. Christmas 3. Devotional exercises. I. Title.
  BV40.H355 2012
  242'.332--dc23

                                                        2012019476

Scripture quotations in this publication, unless otherwise indicated, are from the Common English Bible, © Copyright 2011 by Common English Bible, and are used by permission.

12 13 14 15 16 17 18 19 20 21—10 9 8 7 6 5 4 3 2 1

MANUFACTURED IN THE UNITED STATES OF AMERICA

# Contents

# Introduction

*Scripture: Read John 1:1-18; Genesis 1:1-5*

S tar-watching began as a hobby for Robert Owen Evans. He grew up in a Methodist family in Sydney, Australia. In 1967, he was an ordained minister in the New South Wales Conference where he served as a pastor and studied the history of evangelical movements in the Pacific Islands, Papua New Guinea, Australia, and New York. He retired in 1998 and might have drifted into pastoral obscurity except for his talent for spotting supernovae.

A supernova occurs when a giant star at an incomprehensible distance from the Earth explodes in a spectacular burst of light estimated to be equal in energy to 100 billion suns. That's a lot of light! By the time that light reaches us, it is an unexpected twinkle at a particular spot in the sky that would otherwise be left in darkness.

Pastor Evans began supernova hunting in the 1950's, but he didn't make his first official discovery until 1981. It takes a lot of patience to see something most people don't see. By the end of 2005, he had made forty discoveries. In *A Short History of Nearly Everything*, Bill Bryson records the star-watching pastor saying, "There's something satisfying, I think, about the idea of light traveling for millions of years through space and just at the right moment as it reaches Earth someone looks at the right bit of sky and sees it. It just seems right that an event of that magnitude should be witnessed."[1]

Pastor Evans has trained his eyes to watch empty spaces in the sky so that at just the right moment, by looking at just the right place, he observes a burst of light that the rest of us—too busy to wait, too anxious to watch, too immersed in the present to peer into a light coming from the past—are unprepared and unable to see. He watches and waits for just the right moment when he can be the witness of that moment when a light that has been coming our way for millions of years finally appears.

The writer of the fourth Gospel never could have imagined what Pastor Evans knows about supernovae. Take a moment to look again at John 1:1-18 and Genesis 1:1-5. Compare the use of the word "light" in these Scriptures. How do the Scriptures and the image of light speak to you? John's Gospel bears witness to a light that shines in the darkness, which the darkness has never been able to extinguish. It was, in fact, the light that burst forth in an amazing explosion of light hundreds of millions of years ago on the first day of creation (Genesis 1:3). It was the light through which the world and everything in it came into being. Most of the world, preoccupied with the darkness, didn't recognize the light when it came. But there were some who, like Pastor Evans, became witnesses to that light. They believed it was nothing less than the light of the glory of God in human flesh, leading John to declare, "No one has ever seen God. God the only Son, who is at the Father's side, has made God known" (John 1:18).

Advent is the season in which we watch, wait, and prepare to bear witness to the coming of the true light of God's presence in Jesus Christ. Through worship, Scripture, and prayer, we train our eyes to see what the world never sees so that in the hubbub of the holidays, we are prepared to celebrate a "holy day"—the day when God came down among us in human flesh.

Charles Wesley celebrated the coming of Christ in the Christmas carol "Glory Be to God on High." Lines from the first verse of the carol capture the central theme of this Advent study: "Now God comes down . . . God the invisible appears . . . And Jesus is His Name."[2]

The stargazing pastor said, "It just seems right that an event of that magnitude should be witnessed." In this study, we will meet some of the people who witnessed the miracle of the Incarnation—God becoming flesh in Jesus. I invite you into this study with the expectation that as their stories become our story, we can also become witnesses to the light that the darkness has never been able to overcome. Let's do some Advent stargazing!

1. From *A Short History of Nearly Everything*, by Bill Bryson (Broadway Books, 2003); page 35.
2. From *http://www.hymntime.com/tch/htm/g/b/g/gbgohigh.htm*.

# Zechariah and Elizabeth: Waiting for the Sunrise

## Scripture: Read Isaiah 64:1-3; Luke 1:5-80

"It is not we who choose to awaken ourselves, but God Who chooses to awaken us. . . . Our discovery of God is, in a way, God's discovery of us. We cannot go to heaven to find Him. . . . He comes down from heaven and finds us."

Thomas Merton[1]

Advent begins with a question that haunts the soul of every person with a sensitive heart. We hear it in one of the lessons for the first Sunday in Advent—Isaiah 64:1-3. The prophet Isaiah shakes his fist at the heavens and shouts:

If only you would tear open
   the heavens and come down!
Mountains would quake before you
like fire igniting brushwood
   or making water boil.
If you would make your name known
    to your enemies,
    the nations would tremble in your
    presence.

Most of us know how Isaiah felt, even if we aren't audacious enough to speak it. There are times when we wish God would come down here with something that looks like real power to shake things up and set things right. Faithful people are often tempted to grasp for economic, political, or military power in the hope that by sheer force they can make things right (or at least make things right for their lives, their culture, and their nation), only to be disappointed when the reality they experience falls short of their expectations.

But this is not the way God comes, and it's not the way God makes things right. God comes down in a baby born in a nondescript cow stall in a nowhere place called Bethlehem among powerless people at the bottom of the social, political, and economic ladder. God slips in the back door through the same human sweat and blood by which every one of us is born. God comes down to save this world, not by what the world calls power but by the subversive and often hidden power of self-giving love. We will miss God's coming if we aren't looking in the right place for the right thing. Charles Wesley wrote in his hymn "Glory Be to God on High":

> Glory be to God on high,
> And peace on earth descend;
> Now God comes down, He bows the sky,
> And shows Himself our friend!
> God the invisible appears,
> God the blest, the great I AM,
> He sojourns in this vale of tears,
> And Jesus is His name.[2]

A few years ago in a study I wrote called *Rejoicing in Hope*, I talked about the story of Zechariah and Elizabeth as a couple who "expected the unexpected."[3] In that study, they offered an example of hope in apparently impossible circumstances. Their story also demonstrates much about the way God comes down, to them and to us. The Gospel of Luke tells us three things about them. First, they were both very old. They had lived long enough to experience lives filled with joy and pain, hope and despair, faith and doubt. Second, they were "righteous before God, blameless in their observance of all the Lord's commandments" (verse 6). They had developed a maturing relationship with God that was rooted in the long traditions of God's covenant with Abraham. Third, they had no children.

I have been blessed by the witness of folks like Zechariah and Elizabeth in every congregation I've served. Though none of them would claim to be "blameless," they learned to find God's grace in everything they faced so that their disappointments, pains, and failures became the soil in which new life could grow. They valued the long traditions of the faith without allowing those traditions to become blinders that kept them from seeing the new things God was doing. They have encouraged, challenged, inspired, and guided me along the journey.

Luke tells us that Zechariah and Elizabeth "had no children because Elizabeth was unable to become pregnant" (verse 7). The older translations use the brutal word "barren" to describe Elizabeth's condition. Like Zechariah and Elizabeth, there have been couples in every congregation I have served who have struggled with the challenge of infertility. Waiting and watching with young couples who long to become parents but seem to be unable to, I sometimes find myself shouting at God like Isaiah, "Why don't you come down here and do something about this?" All I can do is walk with them through the long journey of disappointment, of waiting and hoping.

There is more in the story of Zechariah and Elizabeth than just the biological inability to have children. In the Old Testament, the inability to conceive captures the sense of helpless hopelessness in the face of what often feels like the absence of God. For the Hebrew people, the inability to bear children raised the ominous possibility of extinction for their people and an end to the covenant God had made with Abraham. Zechariah and Elizabeth faced a spiritual and theological problem that was even more profound than the biological one.

This story invites us to feel the spiritual emptiness, the soul-level longing, and the desperate hopelessness of the condition Zechariah and Elizabeth faced. They confronted a situation that was beyond their ability or power to change or control. There would be no new life for them without an intrusion of God's presence into the real, tangible stuff of their lives. God came down to them into the midst of their emptiness.

One day when Zechariah was serving in the Temple, the angel Gabriel showed up, standing beside the altar. It frightened the living daylights out of Zechariah, just the way angels always do whenever they show up in the Gospels. And just the way angels always do, the first thing this one said was "Don't be afraid, Zechariah. Your prayers have been heard" (verse 13). Then Gabriel announced the most utterly unexpected and nearly unbelievable promise Zechariah had ever heard: "Your wife Elizabeth will give birth to your son and you must name him John. . . . He will make ready a people prepared for the Lord" (verses 13, 17). The angel's announcement left him unable to speak, but when the baby was born, Zechariah got his voice back and sang like a character in a Broadway musical. The song begins by celebrating what God has done:

> Bless the Lord God of Israel
> because he has come to help
>     and has delivered his people. (verse 68)
> He has raised up a mighty savior for us. . . . (verse 69)
> He has brought salvation. . . . (verse 71)
> He has shown the mercy promised
>     to our ancestors,
>     and remembered his holy covenant. (verse 72)

The song is all about something God has done that Zechariah and Elizabeth never could have done for themselves. That's the point of a baby being born in the geriatric ward. It's also the point of the interwoven story of the unexpected pregnancy of a young girl named Mary who came to visit her relative Elizabeth. We'll miss the point of these pregnancy stories if we get hung up on the biological technicalities in them. Luke's purpose is more theological than it is biological. These stories are more about salvation than they are about obstetrics. God has intersected human history to accomplish God's saving, redeeming purpose for this world in ways that go beyond human power to contain or control. These are not the stories of our journey towards God. They are the shocking stories of God coming down to us to do for us and through us that which we could never do for ourselves.

Advent begins with the awareness that we cannot save ourselves. None of us can give birth to the life, love, joy, and peace that God intends for this creation by our own human power. Our only hope is the radical intrusion of God into this world by God's own power. Zechariah paints a beautiful visual image of this in the final lines of his song:

> Because of our God's deep compassion,
>     the dawn from heaven
>         will break upon us,
>     to give light to those
>         who are sitting in darkness
>     and in the shadow of death,
>         to guide us on the path of peace (verses 78-79).

We can no more cause God to come down to be among us than we can make the sun rise in the morning. But like the supernovae-searching pastor we met in the introduction to this study, we can train our eyes to see the light when it comes. Our task during Advent is to practice the spiritual disciplines that will prepare us to experience the presence of this God who, in deep compassion, comes down to give light to people who live in darkness, to reveal the dawn in the face of death, and to guide us along the pathway of peace.

So what can Zechariah and Elizabeth teach us about being prepared for God to come down to us? For one thing, they teach us the importance of faith that is steeped in the time-tested traditions

of Scripture, worship, and prayer. I often remind my congregation that we can be religious without the Bible and we can be spiritual without the Bible, but we cannot be growing disciples of Jesus Christ without consistent, thoughtful, and prayerful engagement with Scripture. We cannot be prepared to experience God's presence in the present unless we are rooted in what God has done in the past. We recognize God coming into our lives today because we have lived with the story of the way God came into the lives of those who went before us.

Zechariah and Elizabeth also shared a lifelong discipline of worship. In fact, that is what Zechariah was doing when the angel appeared to him. I'm sure there were days when Zechariah wondered what he was doing there, times when he simply seemed to be going through the ritual the way generations before him had done it. But then the day came when an angel appeared and everything was changed.

Advent, which marks the beginning of the liturgical year, is the opportunity to re-energize our commitment to the disciplines of Bible study, personal prayer, and corporate worship. It can also be a time to experience some of the ancient Advent traditions by which saints before us have waited for the coming of Christ.

Thomas Merton entered the Abbey of Gethsemani at the beginning of Advent. He said that he could not imagine a better time to become a monk. "You begin a new life, you enter into a new world at the beginning of a new liturgical year. And everything that the Church gives you to sing, every prayer that you say in and with Christ in His Mystical Body is a cry of ardent desire for grace, for help, for the coming of the Messiah, the Redeemer." He discovered the way the discipline of worship "draws you within . . . where you find God."[4]

Something happened in the Temple that day—something so life-altering that it left old Zechariah speechless. It could be a reminder to us of the importance of silence as one of the ways we prepare for God to enter into our experience. The challenge is that our world hardly knows what to do with silence. And yet, we instinctively know how profoundly we need it.

A lead editorial on "The Joy of Quiet" in *The New York Times* described people who pay $2,285 a night to stay in a cliff-top room at the Post Ranch Inn in California "for the privilege of not having a TV in their rooms." The writer described "the urgency of slowing down—to find the time and space to think," suggesting an "Internet Sabbath" by turning off online connections from Friday evening to Monday morning as a way "of sensing not what's new, but what's essential."[5]

When was the last time you experienced silence? Real silence. The living silence of the earth or sea. With that question, my mind flies across the miles and time that separate me from my first photographic safari to the Masai Mara National Reserve in Kenya. We stood on a cliff looking out across the Great Rift Valley that stretches down through the spine of the African continent. When the vehicles stopped and the engines were shut down, we felt the power of immense silence that was fully alive with the greatness of the earth and utterly devoid of the noise of our hyperactive, mechanized world.

I have experienced the same kind of silence in the Great Smoky Mountains, in a hillside monastery in Kentucky, and along a quiet river in rural Florida. And sometimes, though not often enough, I know that same silence when I am alone in prayer. It's a silence that is pregnant with the presence of God, who gives birth to new life in barren places, new light in the darkness, and new hope in the midst of despair.

We would like God to come down with some display of power that would shake the earth and instantly reorder our lives. But instead, God comes down on a "silent night, holy night" when Christ is born to people who have trained their eyes to see his coming and prepared their hearts to receive him.

A Methodist pastor in South Africa who waited, watched, and worked for 40 years to see freedom come to his land told me about times when things seemed hopeless. During those times, he would cling to the words of a hymn by Henry Burton, "There's a Light upon the Mountains":

There's a light upon the mountains,
And the day is at the spring,
When our eyes shall see the beauty
And the glory of the King:
Weary was our heart with waiting,
And the night watch seemed so long,
But His triumph day is breaking
And we hail it with a song.[6]

The promise to Zechariah and Elizabeth was, of course, fulfilled. The child was born. Zechariah got his voice back and burst into song. In the same way, Christmas will come. Even the Grinch learned that there was no way to stop it. The dawn will come. But the invitation of Advent is to prepare our ears to hear, our eyes to see, and our hearts to experience the way God comes down.

## Questions for Reflection and Discussion

1. How have you experienced the longing expressed in Isaiah 64:1-3?
2. What is your impression of Zechariah and Elizabeth? How do you picture them? In what ways does their story speak to your life?
3. How have you seen or experienced spiritual barrenness? What was it like? As you reflect on this experience, how do you think God was present for you?
4. Read Luke 1:67-79. What images or phrases in Zechariah's song speak most deeply to you? What do they say to you about the presence of God?
5. The study lists three essential disciplines that prepare the way for God to come to us—Scripture, worship, and silence. How have you experienced these disciplines? Which one needs your attention during this Advent season? How will you practice it?

## Prayer

Read or sing Phillips Brooks's carol "O Little Town of Bethlehem." How can Brooks's prayer become a reality for you?

How silently, how silently, the wondrous gift is given;
so God imparts to human hearts the blessings of his heaven.
No ear may hear his coming, but in this world of sin,
where meek souls will receive him, still the dear Christ enters in.
O holy Child of Bethlehem, descend to us, we pray;
cast out our sin, and enter in, be born in us today.
We hear the Christmas angels the great glad tidings tell;
O come to us, abide with us, our Lord Emmanuel![7]

## Focus for the Week

Advent is the time when we prepare ourselves to experience the coming of Christ. During the coming week, practice one spiritual discipline such as prayer, silence, or Scripture reading that will help you open your eyes, your ears, your heart, and your mind to God's presence.

1. From *Thomas Merton: Essential Writings*, selected by Christine M. Bochen (Orbis Books, 2000); pages 60-61.
2. From *http://www.hymntime.com/tch/htm/g/b/g/gbgohigh.htm*.
3. From *Rejoicing in Hope*, by James A. Harnish (Abingdon Press, 2007); page 11.
4. From *The Seven Storey Mountain*, by Thomas Merton (Harcourt Brace Jovanovich, 1948); page 379.
5. From "The Joy of Quiet" in *The New York Times*, by Pico Iyer (January 1, 2012); pages 1, 6.
6. From *http://www.hymntime.com/tch/htm/t/h/e/theresal.htm*.
7. From *The United Methodist Hymnal* (Copyright © 1989 by The United Methodist Publishing House); 230.

# Joseph:
# Faithful Obedience to the Undressed God

## Scripture: Read Matthew 1:18-25

"Jesus is God simplified. God approachable, God understandable, God love-able. . . . Jesus is the last word that can be said about God. . . . The Christian faith is not a set of propositions to be accepted—it is a Person to be followed."

E. Stanley Jones[1]

The provocative title of this week's study comes from a 17th century Anglican priest and poet named George Herbert who wrote:

Hast thou not heard, that my Lord Jesus di'd?
    Then let me tell thee a strange storie.
    The God of power, as he did ride
    In his majestic robes of glorie,
    Reserv'd to light; and so one day
He did descend, undressing all the way.[2]

It's a strange story, all right. The gospel is the shocking story of the way the Almighty God stripped off "his majestic robes of glory" and came down to be Immanuel, God with us, "undressing all the way." Charles Wesley expressed the same idea in the hymn "Glory Be to God On High":

Him by the angels all adored,
Their maker and their king;
Lo, tidings of their humbled Lord
They now to mortals bring;
Emptied of His majesty,
Of His dazzling glories shorn,
Our being's Source begins to be,
And God Himself is born!

See the eternal Son of God
A mortal Son of Man,
Now dwelling in an earthly clod
Whom Heaven cannot contain!
Stand amazed, ye heavens, look at this!
See the Lord of earth and skies
Low humbled to the dust He is,
And in a manger lies![3]

We'll never feel the impact of what happened in Bethlehem until we are shocked by it. The Almighty God came down to be born from Mary's womb—wet, screaming, helpless, and naked in the same way every one of us was born. William Sloane Coffin called Jesus "a window to divinity, a window revealing as much of God as is given mortal eyes to see."[4] Paul affirmed this shocking claim when he pasted a hymn from the life of the early church into his letter to the Philippians:

Though he was in the form of God,
   he did not consider being equal
   with God something to exploit.
But he emptied himself
   by taking the form of a slave
   and by becoming like human beings.
When he found himself
   in the form of a human,
      he humbled himself by becoming
      obedient to the point of death,
   even death on a cross (2:6-8).

You can forget all those loincloth-dressed portrayals of Jesus in Sunday school paintings and Easter dramas. Crucified prisoners hung on the cross as naked as the day they were born, intentionally stripped of every shred of dignity, left with nothing but their naked human flesh. The gospel is the shocking story of God coming down to us, undressing all the way. Charles Wesley captured it in another of his hymns "And Can It Be that I Should Gain?" in the phrase "emptied Himself of all but love."[5]

If this strange story doesn't shock, confuse, or disturb you, the odds are good that you have either heard it so often that you have become anesthetized to it or that you've never really heard it at all. But if it leaves you more than a little confused, you're a lot like Joseph.

When we meet Joseph in Matthew's Gospel, he is totally confused, utterly perplexed, wrestling in the dark about what to believe and what to do about Mary's inexplicable pregnancy. Luke's Gospel is the Christmas Eve candlelight version of the story. It's a more feminine account, told with an emphasis on Mary and Elizabeth. Luke has the shepherds, the angels, and the music and ends with everyone gathered around the manger singing "Silent Night." Matthew's account is a more masculine story, told with an emphasis on Joseph. Jesus is born into a world filled with confusion, tension, and conflict. Herod is frightened and all of Jerusalem with him. You'd be frightened too if a new king was threatening your control. There's nothing more frightening than authoritarian rulers who feel their authority being threatened. The wise men don't have a clue where they are going. And Joseph is perplexed, unable to make sense of any of it. This event simply did not fit in to any of the previous categories by which he defined reality. For Joseph, the whole thing was utterly incomprehensible. "Incomprehensible" is the word Charles Wesley used in one of his lesser-known carols "Let Earth and Heaven Combine":

> Let earth and Heaven combine,
> Angels and men agree,
> To praise in songs divine
> The incarnate Deity,
> Our God contracted to a span,
> Incomprehensibly made Man.
>
> He deigns in flesh t'appear,
> Widest extremes to join;
> To bring our vileness near,
> And make us all divine:
> And we the life of God shall know,
> For God is manifest below.[6]

If we tell the truth, for most of us some of the time and some of us most of the time, there's something about this story that leaves us scratching our heads over the incomprehensible mystery of it all. That's why I love Joseph. That may be one of the reasons he is included in the Christmas story. If there's room for Joseph beside the manger, there may just be room for us.

Joseph is one of the many biblical witnesses who led me to the conviction that honest doubt is not the contradiction of faith but an essential element in a growing faith. Joseph reminds us that we don't need to have all our questions answered before we find our place in the gospel story. Being a follower of Christ does not mean that we have all the answers to all of our questions. It means trusting that as I learn more about myself and about him, my questions will find their own answers.

In his classic book *The Christian Agnostic*, Leslie D. Weatherhead offered an invitation that Joseph probably would have accepted:

> Don't exclude yourself from the fellowship of Christ's followers because of mental difficulties. If you love Christ and are seeking to follow him, take an attitude of Christian agnosticism to intellectual problems at least for the present. . . . only accept those things which gradually seem to you to be true. Leave the rest in a mental box labeled, 'awaiting further light.' In the meantime, join in with us in trying to show and to spread Christ's spirit, for this, we feel, is the most important thing in the world.[7]

I have found Weatherhead's description of the box labeled "awaiting further light" to be immensely helpful, particularly with men like Joseph who are both surprised and grateful for a church in which it is okay to doubt, to question, and to search for a meaningful relationship with Christ. I'm grateful to serve a congregation that has room within it for people like Joseph.

Matthew begins with Joseph scratching his head in confusion over the arrival of this child but that's not where the story ends. Matthew also tells the story of Joseph's faith. Not faith as some intellectual exercise by which we give rational ascent to every affirmation in the creed, but faith as a deep, inner trust in the promise of God and a living, growing, dynamic relationship with God in Christ. Not faith that removes every doubt or question, but faith that sets our lives in a new direction and expresses itself in active obedience to what we understand as the promise of God. It means trusting the story of this intrusive God who comes down to us, undressing all the way.

I think the key to Joseph's story is in verse 24: "When Joseph woke up, he did just as an angel from God commanded." Still scratching his head, still wondering what all this would mean, he obeyed. He took Mary as his wife. In taking his place as the father of Mary's child, Joseph stood in the long line of those for whom faith was not only something they did with their brains, but also something they did with their feet. It was not only about the beliefs they affirmed but also about the way they lived. It was faith that was forged on the anvil of active obedience. That's the way the writer of Hebrews described faith in Chapter 11 of the epistle:

By faith Abel offered a better sacrifice (verse 4)
By faith Noah responded with godly fear (verse 7)
By faith Abraham obeyed when he was called to go out to a place. . . . He went out without knowing where he was going. (verse 8)
By faith he lived in the land (verse 9)
By faith Abraham offered Isaac when he was tested. (verse 17)
By faith Isaac also blessed Jacob and Esau concerning their future. (verse 20)
By faith Jacob blessed each of Joseph's sons (verse 21)
By faith Moses refused to be called the son of Pharaoh's daughter. . . . He chose to be mistreated with God's people (verses 24-25)
By faith he left Egypt (verse 27)
By faith he kept the Passover (verse 28)
By faith they crossed the Red Sea (verse 29)

Like those who went before him, Joseph's faith was refined in the crucible of decisive obedience to what he understood to be God's call in his life. In taking Mary as his wife, Joseph took Mary's child as his own, which meant that the rest of Joseph's life would be intertwined with the life of Jesus. Matthew traces the genealogy of Jesus through "Joseph, the husband of Mary—of whom Jesus was born" (1:16). When Jesus causes a ruckus in Nazareth, the neighbors complain, "Isn't he the carpenter's son?" They write Jesus off as being nothing other than Joseph's son, and Matthew concludes, "They were repulsed by him" (13:55-57). The rest of Joseph's life was defined by the life of Mary's son. But my guess is that even in his obedience, Joseph was still scratching his head at the incomprehensible way God had come down into his life.

I remember a college friend who was a lot like Joseph. He was a highly intelligent student who wrestled with all sorts of questions about his faith and was never satisfied with the simplistic answers some faithful Christians tried to give him. We were talking with one of our professors when my friend asked, "How can I make a commitment to Christ when I don't know all that it will mean?" Our wise professor said, "None of us knows all that it's going to mean, but we know enough to make the commitment to follow Jesus and we spend the rest of our lives finding out what it means." I think that's what happened for Joseph. He knew enough to claim this child as his own. He stepped out in obedience to what he knew and spent the rest of his life discovering all that it would mean.

That's what it means to live by faith. Faith does not mean that we never have any questions or doubts, but it does mean that we have claimed the strange story of the life, death, and resurrection of Jesus to be the central story by which we choose to live our lives. We commit ourselves to follow this One who we believe is "Our God contracted to a span, / Incomprehensibly made man."

Joseph's active obedience resulted in a radical reorientation of his life. Matthew tells us that Joseph was a righteous man. That means he was a Synagogue-attending, law-abiding man. And that's what creates the tension in this story. God's law handed down from Moses said that a woman in Mary's condition should be stoned. With Mary's pregnancy, Joseph faced a situation that ran directly against the grain of everything he had been taught to believe or obey. His love for Mary went against the rules by which he had lived his life, forcing him to begin living by a new set of assumptions.

We all have some basic assumptions by which we live. Sometimes they are the result of our life experience, family, or culture. Sometimes they are rooted in the way we have been taught to read Scripture. They are the rules that govern our behavior. But somewhere along the way, we run into experiences or relationships that force us to question some of those assumptions. Sometimes obeying the way revealed in Jesus will mean that these rules are contradicted by our loyalty to Christ, just the way Joseph's loyalty to the law was superseded by his love for Mary.

The angel told Joseph that his supporting role in the drama of salvation was to take Mary as his wife and to name the child Jesus because he will save people from their sins. And that's what Joseph did. Joseph changed his mind and moved in a totally new direction. In light of God's salvation in Jesus Christ, the old assumptions passed away and everything became new.

For Joseph, God coming down as Jesus was not a pleasant addition to what he already believed. The birth of Jesus called for a radical reorientation in his assumptions that resulted in a radical change in his behavior. It was not an addition to what had been but a new definition of what could be. It was not the reaffirmation of his old assumptions but a total shift in what he believed to be true. The coming of Jesus changed Joseph's plans so that he could participate in God's plan. The Bible calls that obedience.

Biblical obedience means taking action in the present based on what we believe God is doing now and will accomplish in the future. Obedience means that we live our lives in ways that are consistent with the way we believe this world will be when God's kingdom really comes and God's will is fully done on earth as it is in heaven. Obedience means that we become supporting actors in God's drama of salvation.

It's a strange story we tell. It's the strange, shocking, incomprehensible story of the Almighty God who lays aside his majestic robes of glory and descends to be Immanuel, God with us, undressing all the way. It's the strange story of the way ordinary, questioning, doubting folks like Joseph can claim this Christ child as their own. It's the strange story of the way human obedience becomes a part of God's work of salvation in this world. And the strangest thing is that when we experience it, we discover that it's true.

## Questions for Reflection and Discussion

1. Paraphrase George Herbert's poem in your own words. What thoughts do you have about his phrase "undressing all the way"?
2. Read Philippians 2:6-8. How does this passage of Scripture impact your understanding of the Christmas story?
3. How do you picture Joseph? What has been your understanding of his role in the Christmas story?

4. Is there room for doubt in your faith? What are some of the doubts and questions you face? How do you respond to Weatherhead's description of "the Christian agnostic"? How does the image of a box labeled "awaiting further light" help you in dealing with your doubts?

5. What do you see as the relationship between faith and obedience?

6. When have you had an experience or relationship that forced you to change some of your assumptions? What difference did it make?

7. What steps do you need to take to live a more obedient life? What keeps you from taking those steps?

## Prayer

O God, who in coming down to us in Jesus Christ did that which by our human comprehension is incomprehensible, give us faith to follow your Son in the ways in which we know him so that by your Spirit we may know him more deeply and obey him more fully. Amen.

## Focus for the Week

Obedience means that we become supporting actors in the strange drama of God's salvation. Make a list of ways you can take steps to be obedient to God. Choose one thing on your list and do it in the week ahead.

1. From *The Word Became Flesh*, by E. Stanley Jones (Abingdon, 1963); page 37.
2. From *http://www.ccel.org/h/herbert/temple/Bag.html*.
3. From *http://www.hymntime.com/tch/htm/g/b/g/gbgohigh.htm*.
4. From *The Collected Sermons of William Sloane Coffin: Volume 1 —The Riverside Years* (Westminster John Knox Press, 2008); page 257.
5. From *The United Methodist Hymnal*; 363.
6. From *http://www.hymntime.com/tch/htm/l/e/e/leehcomb.htm*.
7. From *The Christian Agnostic*, by Leslie D. Weatherhead (Abingdon, 1965); page 21.

# Mary:
# "Le Point Vierge"

## Scripture: Read Luke 1:26-38

"Advent celebrates the rebirth of hope. . . . And Christmas celebrates the hope of rebirth, for Christ is born that we might be born anew. . . . God comes to earth as a child so that you and I can finally grow up."

William Sloane Coffin[1]

A French phrase caught my attention in the writings of Thomas Merton. Even poorly pronounced, *le point vierge* sounds better in French than its English translation "the virgin point." Merton defined *le point vierge* as the "point at which I can meet God in a real and experimental contact." He said, "This little point of nothingness and of absolute poverty is the pure glory of God in us."[2]

Merton found that phrase in the writings of a Catholic scholar named Louis Massignon, who, in the first half of the 20th century, studied Islamic spirituality and discovered the metaphor in the works of a 10th century Sufi mystic. It also appears in the reflections of the 16th century saint Teresa of Avila. More recently, Kathleen Norris called *le point vierge* the place "where conversion begins in the human heart."[3]

My homespun interpretation is that the virgin point is that place in human experience where God comes down to us, and we discover God's transforming presence in our own lives. It can be any time or place when the Spirit of God begins to do something in us that by all human expectations would be impossible. It's the place where we acknowledge our emptiness, our absolute spiritual poverty. In this place, we know in ways that go beyond human knowing that God is with us.

*Le point vierge* is the place where conversion begins—the place where we say yes to the Spirit of God and allow the love of God in Christ to reshape and redirect our lives. Luke's Gospel takes us to *le point vierge* in the life of an otherwise ordinary, nondescript young woman named Mary.

Luke says Mary was a virgin when Gabriel showed up unexpectedly and said, "Rejoice, favored one! The Lord is with you!" Gabriel might have intended that as good news, but the greeting scared Mary just the way it scared Zechariah. You can forget all those chubby little cherubs on Christmas cards. In the Gospels, angels frighten the living daylights out of people. That's why they always begin by saying, "Don't be afraid" (1:28-30).

Gabriel told Mary, "You will conceive and give birth to a son, and you will name him Jesus" (verse 31). The announcement was as great a shock to Mary as it was when Zechariah heard that Elizabeth would bear a son. Mary asked the question any reasonable, intelligent person would ask, "How will this happen since I haven't had sexual relations with a man?" (verse 34). Gabriel told her it would be a unique work of the Holy Spirit within her because "Nothing is impossible for God" (verse 37).

Mary responded, "I am the Lord's servant. Let it be with me just as you have said" (verse 38). You could call this moment in Mary's experience *le point vierge*. It was the point at which the Spirit of God began to do something in Mary that by all human expectations would have been impossible. The virgin point was when Mary said yes and became part of God's saving work in this world.

So what do we do with a story like that? Let's begin by saying that we will miss the point if we spend all of our time debating the biological details of a virgin conception. Luke is teaching the theology of salvation, not a science class about human conception.

Both Luke's Gospel and the early creeds of the church were looking back on the whole of Jesus' life from this side of the Resurrection. The virgin birth is Luke's way of saying that in Jesus we see the essential character of the Almighty God squeezed into human flesh. It's the gospel way of saying that in the life, death, and resurrection of Jesus, we see Immanuel, God with us, womb to tomb, birth to earth, the cradle to the grave.

The story we tell from Christmas to Easter is the life-transforming story of the way the self-giving love that is the essence of the character of God invaded every corner of human existence. That story begins here at the virgin point in Mary's life, the point of absolute nothingness when Mary says, "I am the Lord's servant. Let it be with me just as you have said" (verse 38). It's the point at which Mary allowed the love of God to become a tangible reality in and through her life.

As I reflected on this theme, another gospel character intruded on my Advent journey. He's not in the cast of the Christmas pageant and doesn't appear on Christmas cards. He showed up like an unexpected guest at Christmas dinner. His name is Nicodemus. In contrast to Mary who was nobody, Nicodemus was somebody. He was a Pharisee, a member of the ruling party in the synagogue. He had education, position, and power. But with everything he had, he came to Jesus because he longed for something more. He was weary of his old life and came to Jesus searching for a new one. He was at the point that Merton described as emptiness and absolute spiritual poverty.

Jesus told him that the only way to experience new life in the kingdom of God is to be born anew, born from above, or born again. The Greek word contains all three meanings. The phrase "born again" takes a lot of abuse in our culture. I heard about a well-bred Bostonian who said that if you are born in Boston, once is enough. Or the cynic who said that the problem with born-again people is that they are twice as big a pain the second time around. But just because the phrase is abused doesn't mean that Jesus wasn't correct when he said, "You must be born anew" (John 3:7).

That seemed just as preposterous to Nicodemus as Gabriel's words seemed to Mary. In fact, he asked the same question that Mary asked: How is it possible? He was thinking of the physical realities of birth when he asked, "How is it possible for an adult to be born? It's impossible to enter the mother's womb for a second time and be born, isn't it?" (3:4).

Poor old Nicodemus. He was a literalist with no imagination. He totally missed the point of Jesus' metaphor. Jesus was talking spirit; Nicodemus was thinking gynecology. Jesus was describing the kingdom of God; Nicodemus was picturing maternity wards. Jesus was speaking figuratively about being born from above or born anew; Nicodemus could only think literally about being born again.

Jesus' answer to Nicodemus was similar to Gabriel's answer to Mary, namely that it's all an intrusive work of the Spirit of God. "I assure you, unless someone is born of water and the Spirit, it's not possible to enter God's kingdom. Whatever is born of the flesh is flesh, and whatever is born of the Spirit is spirit. Don't be surprised that I said to you, 'You must be born anew' " (3:5-7).

You could call it the virgin point in Nicodemus' life, the point at which conversion began. It evidently changed the direction of his life because we see him again at the end of the story assisting Joseph of Arimathea in preparing the naked, broken body of Jesus for burial. John records that "Nicodemus, the one who at first had come to Jesus at night, was there too" (19:39).

What might the virgin point be for us? The truth is that no matter how hard we try to crank up whatever people mean by "the Christmas spirit," none of us is capable of giving birth to the life, love, joy, and peace of Christ by our own power. It is always a work of the Spirit that goes beyond our explanation but not beyond our believing. Our only hope is a new birth by the radical invasion of the Spirit of God. The only thing we can contribute to that new life is our absolute poverty of soul and the availability of a young girl named Mary who said yes.

Sometimes *le point vierge* is a quiet, solitary place in our own souls. Sometimes we experience it in relationship with others. Sometimes it surprises us in the middle of our hectic and chaotic lives. Sometimes it happens when we are confronted with an act of compassion, grace, or peace in this world that can only be explained as a work of God's love becoming flesh among us. Wherever and whenever it happens, it is always an invitation for us, like Mary, to say yes. It's the invitation for us and our world to be born anew, born from above, born again and again and again.

## Questions for Reflection and Discussion

1. How does the phrase "the virgin point" strike you? How have you experienced it in your own life?
2. How do you picture Mary? How has her story been a part of your spiritual journey?
3. What difference does it make for you to see the birth narratives in light of the overall story of the gospel? How does the story of the life, death, and resurrection of Jesus impact your understanding of the Nativity?
4. Read John 3:1-18. What has been your experience with Nicodemus' story? What difference does it make in your understanding of Mary's story?
5. What does it mean for you to be "born again," "born anew," or "born from above"? What does the phrase "born of the Spirit" mean to you?
6. When have you learned to say yes and allowed the love of God to be born anew, born from above, or born again in you?

## Prayer

Almighty God, who entered into the life of Mary and became flesh among us, we give you thanks for the example of her obedience to your will. By your Spirit, give birth to new life in us that, like her, we might become the bearers of your life and love to this world. Amen.

## Focus for the Week

*Le point vierge* is the place where conversion begins, the place where we say yes to the Spirit of God and allow the love of God in Christ to reshape and redirect our lives. Consider ways you can say yes to God each day this week as you move through your daily activities.

1. From *The Collected Sermons of William Sloane Coffin: Volume 2—The Riverside Years* (Westminster John Knox Press, 2008); pages 472-473.
2. From *Thomas Merton: Essential Writings* (Bochen); pages 60-61.
3. From *The Cloister Walk*, by Kathleen Norris (Riverhead Books, 1996); page 205.

# The Innkeeper:
# The Place Where Jesus Is Born

*Scripture: Read Luke 2:1-7*

"We satisfy ourselves by offering Him a stable, and hope that He will not come to be a permanent guest. But He comes. In our work, in our thoughts, in our plans, even in our prayers, there is only a stable for Him and yet He is there."

D.T. Niles[1]

I n the eloquence of the King James Version, Luke tells us that "[Mary] brought forth her firstborn son, and wrapped him in swaddling clothes, and laid him in a manger; because there was no room for them in the inn" (2:7).[2] We imagine No Vacancy signs posted at the front door of every hotel, motel, or bed and breakfast in Bethlehem. There was no room in a little village on the edge of nowhere for a poor pregnant woman and her low-wage, day-laborer husband. No room for Mary's child to be born.

In 1566, Pieter Bruegel set the scene in a typical Flemish village in his painting of *The Numbering at Bethlehem*. Children skate on a frozen pond, workers dig their way through the snow, a brewer pours out the contents of his barrel, a man slaughters a pig, and a crowd gathers around the entrance of an already crowded inn. Unnoticed in the busy crowd, Joseph leads the donkey bearing the pregnant Mary in the direction of an inn in which there will be no room. It's one of the most poignant lines in the story. It has given birth to countless Sunday school dramas in which Mary and Joseph go knocking on doors searching for a place for Jesus to be born and are met with cold rejection from a hard-hearted innkeeper.

Unfortunately, there is no innkeeper in the Gospel accounts. He is a fascinating figment of our Christmas imagination. His presence as a witness to the birth of Jesus is conjured up in Christmas songs, legends, and dramas on the basis of what may be a mistranslation of the final word in the phrase "there was no room for them in the inn."

New Testament scholar Ben Witherington III points out that the word Luke used here, *kataluma*, actually means "guestroom." It's the same word Luke used for the room in which Jesus shared his last Passover supper with his disciples (22:11). It described the upper level room of a typical Palestinian home. By contrast, when Luke described the commercial inn where the good Samaritan left the man who had been robbed and beaten, he used the word *pandocheion* (10:34). Instead of a stable, Witherington contends that Mary and Joseph were given the ground level, rear portion of an ancestral family home where the animals were fed, protected, and housed in the winter.[3]

If Luke was actually describing the upper level guestroom of a family home, how might that impact the story? Could it be that Joseph brought Mary to the home of a relative whose guestroom was already packed with others who "belonged to David's house and family line" (2:4)? Could it be that giving them the downstairs back of the house was the best the family had to offer? Or could it be that due to the questionable nature of Mary's pregnancy, the ashamed relatives wanted to hide her away from view? Or could it be that Joseph's relatives were kosher Jews who knew that the house would become unclean if a woman gave birth inside it? And could it be that this is why Matthew says the wise men "entered the house and saw the child" (2:11)? Or could it be that Joseph's relatives rejected Mary and Joseph?

Whatever we do with the innkeeper and however we translate the text, the important question is whether there is more here than just a sentimental detail in a beautiful story from the past. What if this could be an accurate description of our crowded, confused, chaotic present? What if whatever happened in Bethlehem is also the description of what happens in our own lives? What if there really is no room in this world for Jesus' words amid the confusion of our ceaseless chatter? No room for his subversive kingdom in our political power struggles? No room for his call for peacemaking in our addiction to war? No room for his compassion amid our hard-hearted headlines? No room for Mary's vision of the day when the hungry will be fed and the rich go away empty? No room in our sin-broken world for the angels's promise of peace on earth and goodwill to all?

And what if this is not only our story but also God's story? What if this is the story of the loving God who refuses to honor the No Vacancy signs we erect around our lives—the intrusive God who is determined at all costs to be Immanuel, God with us? What if it draws us into the story of our relationship with the God who is at work to transform the kingdoms of the earth into the kingdom of God?

Thomas Merton may have captured the way this story can speak to us when he wrote, "Into this world, this demented inn, in which there is absolutely no room for Him at all, Christ has come uninvited. . . . It is not the last gasp of exhausted possibilities but the first taste of all that is beyond conceiving."[4]

The story we tell at Christmas is nothing less than the shocking announcement of the God who never stops coming down to search for people like Mary and Joseph through whose lives God's new life, new peace, and new hope can be born. The God we meet at the manger is the God who never stops knocking on the closed doors of our lives in a relentless attempt to come in.

Thinking about that No Vacancy sign, I realized that we all have them. We don't like to admit it. We'd like to convince the world that we have it all together, that there are no empty places in our lives, and that we have everything we need. But the truth is that we all hang No Vacancy signs around dark places in our souls and conflicted corners of our world. There are rooms into which we do not want Jesus to go. None of us really want to acknowledge the vacancy in our souls, the emptiness in our hearts, the hollowness in our compassion, or the shallowness of our hopes.

The gospel is the stark reminder that, like the imaginary innkeeper in Bethlehem, the coming of Christ challenges us to take down our No Vacancy signs, to acknowledge our emptiness, so that Christ can be born anew in our lives and in our world. It's fascinating to me that the New Testament begins with the closed door in Bethlehem and ends with the Risen Christ saying, "Look! I'm standing at the door and knocking. If any hear my voice and open the door, I will come in to be with them, and will have dinner with them, and they will have dinner with me" (Revelation 3:20). It suggests that this relentless love of God never stops knocking on the closed doors of our lives and of our world, always searching for a place for Christ to be born.

When Thomas Merton described his first Christmas in the monastery, he wrote, "The emptiness that had opened out within me, that had been prepared during Advent and laid open by my own silence and darkness, now became filled. And suddenly I was in a new world." He experienced "the sweetness of an infinite love. . . . the sense of the presence of a Person; not exteriorized in space . . . but living in the midst. . . . You know that Christ is born within you. . . . That you are standing on the threshold of infinite possibilities!"[5]

I don't think it's a coincidence that Luke used the same Greek word to describe the guestroom in which there was no room for Jesus to be born and the guestroom in which he shared the Passover with his disciples on the night before he died. The One for whom there was no guestroom in Bethlehem now invites his followers into the guestroom where, as the host at the table, he takes bread, blesses it, breaks it, gives it to them, and says, "This is my body, which is given for you." He takes the cup and says, "This cup is the new covenant by my blood, which is poured out for you" (Luke 22:19-20). In that upper room, around that last Passover table, confronted with the astonishing self-giving love of God in Christ, we are invited to take down the No Vacancy signs and allow Christ to come in. It is the place where the love that became flesh in Jesus becomes flesh in us.

One of my favorite Christmas stories has been told and retold by so many preachers that it has taken on a life of its own. It's the story of a nine-year-old boy named Wally. Wally was larger and slower than the other kids. All the kids liked him because he had a gentle heart and looked out for the smaller kids in the playground. Christmas was coming, and the children were preparing to act out the Nativity story. The teacher cast Wally in the role of the innkeeper because he would only have to remember one line. All Wally had to do was stand at the inn door and say, "No room. Go away."

Christmas Eve came and the play was going well. The shepherds didn't trip on their bathrobes, and the wise men didn't lose their gifts. The angels were managing to keep their wings attached and their halos in place. Mary and Joseph arrived at the inn and knocked on the door. Right on cue, Wally shot back, "No room. Go away." Joseph pleaded, "But sir, we have come a long way, and we are tired from the journey." Again, Wally called out, "No room. Go away." With all the dramatic emotion the nine-year-old Joseph could muster, he pleaded, "But please, my wife is having a baby. Don't you have a room where the baby can be born?" There was silence as Wally stared at Joseph and Mary. Everyone in the audience wanted to help Wally remember his forgotten line. Finally, the teacher called in Wally's line from backstage. The young Joseph put his arm around Mary, which was a feat of dramatic training for a young boy. Sadly, they began to walk off the stage. But it was more than Wally's kind heart could take. He shouted after them, "Wait! You can have my room."

Charles Wesley captured the shocking reality of the way God comes down to take up residence in our lives when he wrote these words in "Savior, and Can It Be":

Savior, and can it be
That Thou shouldst dwell with me?
From Thy high and lofty throne,
Throne of everlasting bliss,
Will Thy majesty stoop down
To so mean a house as this?

I am not worthy, Lord,
So foul, so self-abhorred,
Thee, my God, to entertain
In this poor polluted heart:
I am a frail sinful man!
All my nature cries, Depart!

Yet come, Thou heav'nly guest,
And purify my breast;
Come, Thou great and glorious King,
While before Thy cross I bow;
With Thyself salvation bring,
Cleanse the house by entering now.[6]

There may not be an innkeeper in the gospel, but because he is so much like so many of us, he continues to haunt our Advent journey.

William Sloane Coffin preached a Christmas season sermon to the congregation at The Riverside Church in New York City in which he imagined the innkeeper as being "less mean than hassled by all the guests." Perhaps Joseph woke him up in the middle of the night, asking for a place where the child could be born. Perhaps rather than simply turn them away, he led them to the stable, pulled down some fresh hay, and offered them a blanket to ward off the cold. Coffin suggested that when the shepherds came, the innkeeper was probably just as happy to send them to the stable because "shepherds can smell up an inn like a skunk in a woodshed." And when Joseph fled in the middle of the night to escape Herod's wrath, the innkeeper was probably grateful that he hadn't taken them in. Coffin imagined that the innkeeper prospered in his work, opened a few more inns, and thirty years later found himself living in a comfortable house in the city of Jerusalem. He wondered if the innkeeper ever thought back on that night and questioned what became of that child.

One day a friend asked the innkeeper if he had heard of Jesus of Nazareth. The innkeeper said that he had and was quite impressed with what he heard. Then, to the innkeeper's surprise, his friend asked if he realized that Jesus was the baby who was born behind his inn in Bethlehem. Suddenly it all came back to the innkeeper— the mother's cry, the star in the sky, the shepherds, and the wise men. At that point in the story, Coffin said, "He knows that while tragic errors remain tragic, no tragedy has to remain pure tragedy, for as no sin is beyond God's forgiveness, the past is never beyond redemption." He pictured the innkeeper sending Jesus a message to invite him to knock on his door a second time.

In Coffin's imagination, the nameless "owner of the house" in Luke 22:11 is none other than the innkeeper from Bethlehem. He said, "I like to picture him standing in the door watching Jesus break and distribute the bread. And when he saw Jesus take the cup, and heard him say that his blood would be poured out for the forgiveness of many, he shed tears of gratitude." And so, Coffin told his congregation, "Remember the innkeeper, remember that no sin is beyond forgiveness, no past beyond redemption."[7] The gospel is the story of the relentless intrusion of God's love that refuses to acknowledge the No Vacancy signs we post around our lives. It means that there is always hope for every one of us. Is there room in your life for Christ to be born?

## Questions for Reflection and Discussion

1. Find Bruegel's painting *The Numbering at Bethlehem* online. If you set this story today, how would you picture the scene?
2. How do you respond to Witherington's explanation of the Greek words for "inn" and "guestroom"? What difference does it make in your understanding of the story?
3. What are some of the No Vacancy signs in your life or in

our world? Name some of the doors we would prefer to keep closed to the presence of Christ. How would you name the vacancy or emptiness in your life?

4. Reread Merton's description of his experience at the monastery. When have you experienced something similar?

5. Read Luke 22:7-13. How do you feel about the connection between the guestroom in Bethlehem and the guestroom where Jesus shared the Last Supper? What does it mean for you to celebrate Holy Communion at Christmas?

6. How does Coffin's imaginary story of the innkeeper connect with you? Imagine the way you would tell the story from the innkeeper's perspective. Is there something in your past that needs to be forgiven or redeemed?

## Prayer

Rewrite Wesley's hymn "Savior, and Can It Be" in your own words and use it as your prayer.

## Focus for the Week

The gospel is the timeless story of the relentlessly loving God who refuses to honor the No Vacancy signs we erect around our lives—the intrusive God who is determined at all costs to be Immanuel, God with us. Reflect on how God might be ignoring a No Vacancy sign in your daily life in order to be with you.

1. From *The Power At Work Among Us*, by D.T. Niles (Epworth Press, 1967); page 124.
2. Scripture quotations from The Authorized (King James) Version. Rights in the Authorized Version in the United Kingdom are vested in the Crown. Reproduced by permission of the Crown's patentee, Cambridge University Press.
3. From *http://www.bib-arch.org/e-features/nativity.asp*.
4. From *A Thomas Merton Reader*, edited by Thomas P. McDonnell (Doubleday, 1974); pages 365, 367.
5. From *A Thomas Merton Reader* (McDonnell); pages 156-157.
6. From *http://hymntime.com/tch/htm/s/c/a/scanitbe.htm*.
7. From *The Collected Sermons of William Sloane Coffin: Volume 2—The Riverside Years*; pages 476-477.

# A Witness to Wonder

### Scripture: Read Isaiah 9:2-7

"God is not confined to Christ, only most essentially defined by Christ. . . .
What is finally important is not that Christ is Godlike, but that God is Christ-like.
God is like Christ. That's what we need to know."

William Sloane Coffin[1]

I hear the same thing every year. In what I am sure is an attempt to at least be sympathetic with the plight of the preacher preparing for Christmas Eve, someone will say, "It must be hard to come up with a new Christmas sermon every year. It's always the same story." They are correct, of course. There's only one story to tell at Christmas, the story that has given birth to more stories than any other story. But it's the story that never grows old, the story that is never exhausted in the telling, a story that always contains more than we can draw from it.

In the fourth century, John Chrysostom was the preacher everyone wanted to hear. In a Christmas sermon that has become a classic, he said that the story of the birth of Christ should not "be probed too curiously with wordy speech." I'm not sure that's what one of my staff members had in mind when, as we headed into the sanctuary on Christmas Eve, he advised me, "Keep it short." In this same sermon, Chrysostom went on to say:

What shall I say! And how shall I describe this Birth to you? For this wonder fills me with astonishment. The Ancient of days has become an infant. He Who sits upon the sublime and heavenly Throne, now lies in a manger. And He Who cannot be touched . . . now lies subject to the hands of men . . . God is now on earth, and man in heaven.[2]

"What shall I say!" That's where every preacher begins, not because there is so little to say, but because what needs to be said is beyond the ability of our language to convey. And yet, the story is so simple that a child can tell it.

I've seen the Nativity performed in the splendor of the Radio City Christmas Spectacular. I've heard it read by movie stars with massed choirs at The Walt Disney World Resort. I've seen it celebrated in gothic cathedrals. But it's hard to beat the way preschool-age children tell it with angels in tinsel halos, shepherds in bathrobes, and wise men in Burger King crowns. That's particularly true if one of those wise men happens to be your own three-year-old grandson!

Organizing a cast of preschoolers is a lot like herding cats. The exhausted teachers were clearly ready for their Christmas break to begin. They did their best to keep things in order, but the production had its share of children roaming around, halos coming loose, and cardboard crowns slipping down in front of wise men's faces.

The girl playing Mary was supposed to be standing in prayerful adoration beside the manger as the narrator read the story. But she noticed that the blanket around the plastic baby had come undone. Oblivious of anything else that was going on, she did what any responsible mother would do. She picked up the naked baby and held him somewhat precariously in one arm while she took the blanket from the manger and spread it out on the floor. She gently laid the baby down and carefully wrapped the blanket around it. No baby was ever more lovingly swaddled than this one. She picked the baby up, placed him on her shoulder, patted his back, and rocked him there while the rest of the children sang:

Jesus our brother, kind and good
Was humbly born in a stable rude
And the friendly beasts around Him stood,
Jesus our brother, kind and good.[3]

For a preschool Mary, that plastic baby might as well have been the real one, born in flesh and blood and in need of a good burping in Bethlehem.

Then our attention turned to the five-year-old girl who played the angel who announced the birth to the shepherds. Most of the parents knew that her father and uncle had both been killed in a horrible automobile accident just a few months before. My daughter was not the only person in the room who wiped a tear from her eye when, with all of the gusto a preschool girl could muster, the now fatherless angel shouted, "Behold, I bring you good news of a great joy. To you is born this day in the city of David a Savior who is Christ the Lord."

In that moment, I couldn't help but think that's just how real this story is. The good news of great joy is proclaimed in a world where preschool children sometimes lose their fathers, where parents sometimes lose their jobs, and where families sometimes lose their homes. The angels sing of "peace on earth and goodwill to all" in a world where Herod still reigns and where nations still believe the myth that peace can be purchased through war. God comes down in flesh into a world where love still gets nailed to a cross. The Savior is born in a world where every last one of us is like those lost, confused, disoriented shepherds who are in desperate need of a Savior.

We began our journey through Advent with the Old Testament prophet Isaiah shouting at God, "If only you would tear open the heavens and come down!" (Isaiah 64:1). And who among us, if we tell the truth about what we feel, hasn't felt that way? Who among us has not wanted to shout, "Why don't you get real, God? Why don't you get down here and do something about the mess we've made of things?"

In the manger in Bethlehem, we see the astonishing way God answered Isaiah's plea, again in the words of Isaiah: "A child is born to us, a son is given to us" (9:6). Charles Wesley's hymn "Glory be to God On High," which we saw in Chapter 1, echoes and responds to Isaiah's plea:

> Glory be to God on high,
> And peace on earth descend;
> Now God comes down, He bows the sky,
> And shows Himself our friend!
> God the invisible appears,
> God the blest, the great I AM,
> He sojourns in this vale of tears,
> And Jesus is His name.[4]

The good news of the gospel is not that Jesus came to show us the way to climb up to God, but that God came down to us, descending into the real stuff of our real lives—God with us in Jesus Christ.

> Grace invaded gravity.
> Infinite love became finite creation.
> The limitless God entered our human limitations.
> Unbounded life was bound in a baby blanket and laid in a manger.

God did not come down to earth in Jesus Christ to make life just a little bit better but to save us from existence that is less than life into real life itself. God came down in Jesus not to prepare us for the next world but to set us free to live in this world the way Jesus lived, which was the costly way of reconciling love, relentless hope, reverberating joy. God came down to live with us so that we could live like him. God came down to save us from violence by showing us the way of peace. To save us from greed by showing us the way of compassion. To save us from our addiction to narrow self-interest by showing us the way of self-giving love. To save us from sin by showing us the way to forgiveness. To save us from death by showing us the way to life. To save us from sorrow by showing us the way of joy.

I have a friend who, like many of my friends, has been going through a very difficult time. His business tanked in the economic recession. His mother drifted into total dementia. His father had a very difficult time coping with that and descended into a major depression. My friend has faced health challenges in his own family. There were plenty of times when he felt like shouting, "God! Why don't you get down here and do something?" Just a few days before Christmas, I received an email in which he wrote:

> God and I are getting along a lot better now. I'm still not very happy about the way He allows things to happen, but in all of this He and I have become much closer. Jesus is with me, living within me, standing beside me. He never lets go. My faith is stronger than ever, leading me, giving me strength. More than ever the Christmas message of Christ coming to us where we are, being born among us, being born within us, is at the center of who I am. Merry Christmas!

Explain that? You've got to be kidding. It goes beyond rational explanation and into the realm of experience.

Zechariah, Elizabeth, Joseph, Mary, the innkeeper—one thing all these witnesses to the incarnation have in common is the wonder and mystery of a God whose love is utterly incomprehensible to our minds but totally accessible to our experience. The subsequent verses of Wesley's hymn express this wonder and mystery:

> See the eternal Son of God
> A mortal Son of Man,
> Now dwelling in an earthly clod
> Whom Heaven cannot contain!
> Stand amazed, ye heavens, look at this!
> See the Lord of earth and skies
> Low humbled to the dust He is,
> And in a manger lies!

So do the sons of men rejoice
The Prince of Peace proclaim,
With Heaven's host lift up our voice,
And shout Immanuel's name;
Our knees and hearts to Him we bow;
Of our flesh, and of our bone,
See—Jesus is our Brother now,
And God is all our own![5]

There is a time for explanations, but Christmas isn't one of them. We come to worship and experience the mystery, to kneel in humble awe before the wonder of a God who loves this world enough to come down, all the way down, to save it.

I suspect that Robert Owen Evans, who I mentioned in the introduction to this study, is out there tonight, staring into the Australian sky, waiting to be a witness to the wonder of light breaking through the darkness. Given the wonder of the way God came down to us in Jesus, "it just seems right that an event of that magnitude should be witnessed."[6] Like the witnesses with whom we have spent these weeks of Advent, may each of us become a witness to the wonder of the way God came down to us in Jesus.

## *Questions for Reflection and Discussion*

1. Reread the words by John Chrysostom. When have you experienced the kind of wonder he described?
2. How do you respond to the story of the preschool Nativity? What memories do you have of similar presentations of the Christmas story? How do you reconcile the Christmas story with the losses you have faced in your life?
3. How much space is there in your faith for mystery and wonder? How important is it for you to have rational explanations of every element of the faith?
4. What does it mean for you to say that God came down in Christ to "save" us?

5. When have you had an experience of Christmas that left you in sheer amazement at the meaning of the Incarnation?

6. What have you learned or experienced during this study that will make a difference in your life in the year ahead?

## *Prayer*

Almighty God, the source of all life and light,
    when darkness covered the earth
    you spoke the word and brought forth light.
When we wandered in the darkness of our own folly and sin,
    you sent the light that shines in the darkness
    which the darkness will never overcome.
Lead us out of the darkness into the bright dawn of your new life
    in Jesus Christ
    that we might become the light of the world,
    faithful in word and deed until the dawn breaks
    and the whole earth reveals your glory.
Through Jesus Christ, the light among us,
Amen.

## *Focus for the Week*

The great good news of the gospel is not that Jesus came to show us the way to climb up to God, but that God came down to us, descending into the real stuff of our real lives—God with us in Jesus Christ. Offer a prayer of gratitude each day for God's willingness to come down to us in Jesus Christ.

1. From *The Collected Sermons of William Sloane Coffin: Volume 1—The Riverside Years*; page 257.
2. From *http://prydain.wordpress.com/2006/12/07/st-john-chrysostom-homily-on-christmas-morning/*.
3. From *http://www.hymnsandcarolsofchristmas.com/Hymns_and_Carols/friendly_beasts.htm*.
4. From *http://www.hymntime.com/tch/htm/g/b/g/gbgohigh.htm*.
5. From *http://www.hymntime.com/tch/htm/g/b/g/gbgohigh.htm*.
6. From *A Short History of Nearly Everything*, (Bryson); page 35.

Made in United States
Orlando, FL
18 October 2022

23614405R00029